The New Beetle

Ivan McCutcheon

BARNES
&NOBLE
BOOKS
NEW YORK

This edition published by Barnes & Noble, Inc., by arrangement with Carlton Books Limited

1999 Barnes & Noble Books

M 10 9 8 7 6 5 4 3 2 1

ISBN 0-7607-1398-7

Editor: Tim Dedopulos
Senior Art Editor: Zoë Maggs
Designer: Brian Flynn
Picture Research: Lorna Ainger
Production: Alexia Turner

Printed & Bound in Dubai

ACKNOWLEDGEMENTS

Without the help of Volkswagen, in Germany, America and Britain, this book would not have been possible. Special thanks go to Tony Fouladpour at *VW of America* Public Relations, who was a great help with Concept 1 and Concept Cabriolet, Rüdiger Folten of the Design and Strategy department at *Volkswagen AG Germany*, who gave me a fantastic insight into the design of the New Beetle, and Alison Kempster and Paul Bucket of the *Volkswagen UK* press office, for all their efforts. Thanks also to Dean Kirsten, Technical Editor of *Dune Buggies and Hot VWs Magazine*, Mike Pye for loaning me his Apple Mac, Nigel Fryatt, *VolksWorld*'s Publisher, for granting me permission to write this book, Keith Seume, total VW-head and prior Editor of *VolksWorld*, for his help over the years, and David West, of parts specialist *German and Swedish* in London, England, for handing over the keys to his New Beetle for a four day road test which saw just under 1000 miles added.

The New Beetle

Ivan McCutcheon

BARNES
&NOBLE
BOOKS
NEW YORK

Contents

Introduction

The world-renowned VW Beetle was designed by Ferdinand Porsche during the 1930s. It

rose from the ashes after World War II in a truly amazing fashion, against formidable odds.

The car persevered during its early years of production to finally become established as the

world's best-selling car to date.

The car's success was due to three main factors – good world wide sales, excellent service back up, and the craft with which it was advertised by Doyle Dane Bernbach. The campaigns were honest and never over-promoted the car. The virtues of build quality, durability, reliability, economic ownership, and superb after-sales back up were presented in simple terms and the car sold in great numbers.

The dash features a flower vase

Soon the VW wasn't the oddest looking car on the block – it blended in with all the other Beetles. With a production figure which currently stands at over 22,000,000 it is no surprise the Beetle is the most easily recognisable automobile in the world.

Most of us have had some kind of contact with a Beetle, whether that be having owned one or more, travelled in one, known someone who owns one or, in quite a few cases, having been born in one! There are innumerable Beetle tales in countless countries and a myriad of memories, both good and bad, about these quirky cars.

The original Beetle was masterful in any weather conditions

Today the Volkswagen Beetle is one of the few classic vehicles you are still likely to see in use in significant numbers on a daily basis. This car has the largest enthusiast following of any model, and the most single brand monthly publications devoted to it. In addition, it still supports the largest after-market parts and maintenance industry bar none. By 1966 in the United States alone Volkswagen and its distributors and dealers employed over 29,000 staff. If this figure were to be added to the numbers of people in the unofficial support work force which have made a living selling parts and maintaining the vehicle, it could easily be doubled.

On the open road, the New Beetle turns heads

With such a fantastic record it was no surprise that the public and press went wild about the VW concept car for the 1994 Detroit Motor Show. The New Beetle has gone on to give the company more good press than any other model it has made. Since being launched on January 5th 1998, the New Beetle has been on more front covers and television screens than any new car in recent times. This has created mayhem for the dealers and must be quite upsetting to other manufacturers – after all, Volkswagen has gone and done it again!

What remains to be seen is whether the public interest will burn out or keep going, as the new VW Beetle has not yet been officially launched in many markets. It is uncertain whether this very trendy car will be 'in' for a short time or whether it will sell for decades like its older brother did. Previous VW advertising claimed the Beetle fad had died out as so many had been sold that it wasn't a unique car any longer – but even this didn't stop sales.

We will look into what has happened with the VW Beetle so far, from the Concept 1 vehicle at Detroit through to the launch of the New Beetle. We will also explore the factory where it is built and take a look at the way the car has been such a successful exercise for VW. The future will take its own course, and no doubt there will be many more interesting chapters in the life of this great little car. My only regret is I can not cover acts which have not yet taken place.

I have never seen myself as a soothsayer, but I feel this fantastic car is the Millennium Bug we would be only to happy to own! If you are one of those who have already taken delivery of a New Beetle I hope you enjoy every moment you have together. After all, you are driving not only one of the most talked-about new cars of the decade, but a piece of automotive history in the making!

VW has come up with a unique car again!

1

The VW 30 prototype from the front and rear

Heritage

The in-depth history of the Beetle has been covered in many publications, but there will be

a number of new enthusiastic owners who have become interested in the car's history and

heritage solely through the New Beetle. Although this book focusses on the New Beetle, we

will take a brief look at the Beetle's history in the same way VW looked to its roots for the

basic theme of this sensational car.

The Beetle was originally designed by Dr. Ferdinand Porsche. The first prototype car which bore any resemblance to the Beetle was the Porsche Type 32, built in 1933 for NSU. This car had a very similar shape, an air-cooled four cylinder boxer engine (horizontally opposed pairs of cylinders) mounted at the rear and displacing 1470cc, linked to a swing-axle transmission. It also featured the Porsche-designed front and rear torsion bar suspension systems, which would go on to be used on the Beetle. This prototype would never actually see production as a proper vehicle, but it proved to be a valuable exercise for what lay ahead.

At the beginning of 1933, Ferdinand Porsche met with the new Chancellor of Germany, Adolf Hitler, to discuss the Auto-Union racing car he was working on at the time. The meeting was to request that the funding of the car be supplied by the government, and everything went according to plan.

When Hitler decided he wanted to mobilise the German population at all levels, and not just those wealthy enough afford the luxury of a motor car, he needed someone to design the vehicle. His thoughts turned to Dr. Porsche. Ironically enough, Porsche had already been trying to get a Peoples car into production, having had the same idea.

The VW 38 prototype from 1938 was basically the same as the car that went into production

Porsche was asked to put his ideas down on paper and submit them for review. The main recommendations of the paper, which was presented in January 1934, were that the car should be built to a very high standard, but also be low priced. The car should not be under-powered, and should not be a small car but a four-seater hardtop with the best possible handling and suspension, able to reach a maximum cruising speed of around 100Km/h and have a climbing ability of around 30 per cent. Porsche also stressed the vehicle should be simple to maintain and cheap to run.

In May 1934 Porsche was asked to meet with Hitler in Berlin. At this meeting, Dr. Porsche discovered that Hitler liked what he had read. He wanted Porsche to produce a Peoples car which had the ingredients Porsche had suggested – for the price of a motorcycle!

Though he felt it was impossible to meet these requirements, Porsche made designs for a prototype vehicle. This became known as the Porsche Type 60, and he submitted it for Hitler's approval. The

This 1950 Beetle shows how little was changed from the VW 38. Note that the front turn signals are later additions

design was passed and handed over to the R.D.A, a governing body for the vehicle manufacturing industry. Porsche was contracted to develop the People's car in June 1934.

Porsche was given a grant to produce three working prototypes from the Type 60 design, but by today's standards the amount he was given was farcical. However, Porsche took the contract and the grant. The three prototypes were given Verusch (experimental) type designations V1 and V2.

By October 1935 the prototypes were being built in secret and, although a little behind schedule, they were ready for testing. There were a few mechanical problems which appeared during rigorous daily testing in excess of 400 miles, but generally the car proved to be satisfactory.

Hitler then passed control of the Peoples car project to the DAF, the German workers front. He charged the German workers an extra 1.5 per cent tax and set up a fund for the project which he called the Society for the development of Volkswagens or, to use the German abbreviation, 'Gesuvor'.

Although this enforced finance deal was a bit underhand, it provided funds to produce further prototypes, known as the VW 30, in early 1937. These prototypes were actually produced by Daimler Benz and looked similar to the car which we know as the Beetle. The prototypes were tested by 120 SS servicemen over more than a million and a half miles – a feat unheard of at the time. With such rigorous testing, any problems would certainly have been found and fixed.

1938 saw the Volkswagen Beetle in the final stages of development with the production of 44 VW 38 prototypes. In February, Adolf Hitler ordered the head of the Gesuvor, Dr Bodo Lafferentz, to locate an area in which to build a production factory for the Peoples Car. The ideal site required enough surrounding land for workers' accommodation. The area he chose was Fallersleben, and the town is now known as Wolfsburg, close to the Mittelland Canal and the Autobahn between Hanover and Berlin.

Strength Through Joy

The factory site was under construction by February 1938 and on May 26th, Adolf Hitler attended a lavish ceremony where he officially unveiled the new prototype cars and also laid the foundation stone of the factory. At this point the factory and town were not known as Wolfsburg, but the Kraft-durch-Freude Stadt, or Strength Through Joy Town. If you wonder exactly what that is supposed to mean, you'll be thinking along the same lines as Dr Porsche was when he heard Hitler announce the name for the vehicle. It was not going to be the People's car, or Volkswagen, but it would be called the KdF-wagen, or Strength Through Joy car! Despite the fact that the name was really rather silly, sounding odd even in the original German, from May 26th the car was officially known as the KdF-wagen!

1953 saw the oval rear window

The Kdf-wagens were then driven around Germany and shown off to the public. A KdF savers' scheme was set-up by Dr Robert Ley, head of DAF. The idea was you simply bought stamps and stuck them onto cards. When you had saved enough stamps, you got your car. It didn't work quite that smoothly. In reality, you expected to get your car and then started waiting – hundreds of thousands of Germans entered the scheme and not one got a KdF-wagen.

During 1939, construction of the factory was going very well indeed, and by April the American-made machinery was arriving and being fitted. However, the outbreak of World War II stopped work on the factory. It had yet to produce a car. By the end of the year, the factory had made a loss equivalent to two million dollars! Throughout the war years, from 1940 to 1945, the unfinished factory pro-

duced military vehicles based mainly on KdF-wagen mechanicals, also designed by Porsche. In total 50,788 Kübelwagens and 14,276 amphibious Schwimmwagens were made in 1940. By the end of the war just 630 Kdf-wagens were produced. Many of these were strictly for high ranking Nazi party members, or for use in the field.

Above: the Oval window
Main pic: from August 1957, the 'Big window'

The British Years

Production of military vehicles made the factory a target for the allied bombers. By 1944, two thirds of it had been destroyed in daylight bombing raids. However, as the factory's facade was over a mile long, production continued despite the poor conditions.

At the end of the war, the allies took control of all German industry and the Volkswagen factory was put under the control of the British army. Under the command of Colonel Charles Radcliffe, and Colonel Michael McEvoy of the Royal Electrical and Mechanical Engineers, poverty stricken locals were given the task of clearing up the damaged factory and repairing allied vehicles and rebuilding engines. The Beetle production machinery was found, taken out of storage, and two Beetles were constructed by hand so that the car could be evaluated.

Although the Beetle persevered, if received a mixed reception. Apart from those at the factory, including REME Major Ivan Hirst, no-one seemed to think very much of the car. A leading British motor manufacturer, Humber, evaluated the Volkswagen and thought it was a waste of time saying, 'It does not meet the fundamental technical requirements of a motor car. As regards to performance and design, it is quite unattractive to the average motor car buyer. It is too ugly and too noisy. To build the car commercially would be a completely uneconomic enterprise.' According to Humber, the future of the Beetle looked bleak. The officers of REME had faith, however. During 1945 the Volkswagen town was renamed Wolfsburg, and the factory was called the Wolfsburg Motor Works.

In early 1946 Wing Commader Dick Berryman, the production engineer, was given orders by Radcliffe to get the Volkswagen factory working again. By March 1946 the factory had produced 1000 units and by the end of the year, nearly 8000 had been built and given the designation Type 11. These vehicles were destined for occupying forces, known as The Control Commission for Germany. The factory had also been producing Kübelwagens and various variants from spare parts, again for the C.C.G.

An uncertain future?

In 1947, Major Hirst was given permission to sell Volkswagens to British servicemen. This was followed by perhaps the most significant step towards the future of VW – the managing officers at the factory decided to exhibit the Volkswagen at the Hannover Trade Fair. For the first time, the German public could actually buy the car, even though few had enough money. In addition, this important move successfully secured a contract with the Pon brothers from the Netherlands, who were to be the first VW dealers and importers.

At this stage the future of the factory was still not certain, and by the end of 1947 the British were looking for a German to take control of Wolfsburg. Major Hirst eventually managed to track down the right man, Heinz Nordhoff, and as the future would prove, appointing this man as Managing Director secured the future success of Volkswagen.

By May 1948, 25,000 Volkswagens had been produced. Volkswagen also exported vehicles – 23% of its production was shipped to Luxembourg, Belgium, Switzerland, Denmark and Sweden, bringing in valuable foreign currency. In Germany Volkswagen accounted for over half the cars built, and in 1948, a total of 19,244 cars were built in total that year. Nordhoff had created service and sales organisations wherever the VW was sold, and this became the foundation of the world wide success of the VW. In 1949 the C.C.G. control of Volkswagen was relinquished and the Federal Government was given control of the operation.

Nordhoff arranged for Ben Pon to take the first VW to the U.S.A, to be displayed at a German Industrial Exhibition in New York. However, the car was not greeted with much enthusiasm and Pon ended up selling it to pay for his hotel bill before returning to Europe. This was bad news for Nordhoff, as he wanted to break into the largest car market in the world and obtain US Dollars to fund further purchases of machinery.

This situation changed in the middle of the fifties, as the American market looked beyond massive highly-chromed vehicles with powerful engines. The Volkswagen Beetle came across as a class-free and unconventional car which had no non-essential extras. This contrasted with the American vehicles, which typically had extensive electrical specifications, and included power steering, powered windows, power seats and sometimes even powered convertible roofs. With the Beetle, less was more, which appealed to individualists and those not able to afford the monsters Detroit had thrived on.

Sales take off

The bonus of owning a VW was that it looked the same every year, unlike the American cars which the manufacturers changed every year in a competition for customers. So if you bought a Beetle and kept it a few years most people wouldn't even know what year the car had been made. Parts were readily available, through the huge dealer network which had been formed. Service bills were cheap, and the Beetle was a very reliable car. It was no surprise that the word started to get around!

Official sale started in Britain in 1953. Surrey-based motor trader John Colborne Baber had been bringing used Beetles into Britain since 1948 and dressing them up with chrome trim and vinyl interiors. Many of these Beetles were converted to right-hand drive. Official imports didn't start until 1953, when the ban on car imports, set after World War II, was released.

In 1955 the Millionth Beetle rolled of the Wolfsburg production line, and by 1959 Volkswagen was producing over 575,000 Beetles a year. The waiting list in the U.S.A. was up to six months. In 1960 Volkswagen reached another landmark – 500,000 Beetles had been sold in the U.S.A.

This was an amazing achievement when you consider the fact the company hadn't seriously advertised the car! When VW did, sales soared even further, mainly thanks to the ideas of Doyle Dayne Bernbach. The advertising was honest, unpretentious and fun. DDB's technique made prospective customers feel they were being addressed sensibly and on their own level, rather than bragging that life would be more glamorous if they owned a Beetle. Consequently, 1962 saw the 5 millionth VW produced and annual production up to a million. In 1963 VW opened the headquarters of Volkswagen of America in Englewood Cliffs, New Jersey.

In 1964, Volkswagen formed VW de Mexico S.A. de C.V in Peubla, Mexico and started building VWs to German standards at low prices for local consumption. This was one of many factories worldwide which produced Beetles either from scratch or from kits sent from Germany. Peubla went on to play a very large part in the story of the New Beetle. By 1965, 10 million Volkswagens had been pro-

The 50th Year Beetle from 1985 was built in Mexico

duced. In February 1972, VW took over the record for highest production of a vehicle from the Ford Model T, with the 15,007034th Beetle. The cars continued to roll off the production line.

After some 30 years, the Wolfsburg factory ceased Beetle production in 1974 to make way for the new VW Golf. However the Beetle was still built in several places – including Emden in Germany, Belgium, Peubla in Mexico, South Africa, Brazil, Australia, The Philippines, Uruguay, Nigeria, Malaysia, Peru, Venezuela and Indonesia! On the 19th of January 1978, the last Beetle to be built in Europe rolled of the line at Emden, although Mexican imports were still brought in to Europe. On the 15th of May 1981, the 20 millionth Beetle was built in Mexico. Beetles were shipped into Germany until August 1985, by which time demand had dropped, and imports became uneconomical. Production didn't cease though, and in June 1992 numbers were up to 21 million. Today the air-cooled Beetle is still in production at Peubla, and over 22 Million have been produced.

The Beetle has the strongest following of any car. There are over a thousand enthusiast clubs world wide, and hundreds of VW-only car meetings are held each year. There are countless unofficial after-market parts manufacturers, stores, and service and restoration companies. No model has been more written about, customised, raced, tuned or restored to perfection. It is without a doubt the most popular classic car ever produced, and the amazing thing is that is still in production today.

2

Concept 1

Concept 1 and a 1946 Beetle, by Dean Kirsten

When the doors of the North American International Motor Show in Detroit, Michigan

opened to the motoring press in January of 1994, Volkswagen of America provided a real

shock to the motor world in the shape of something very close to being familiar. It was the

design study known as Concept 1, the vehicle presented to the world by Ulrich Seiffert, head

of Research and Development at Volkswagen.

However, the story starts long before the 1994 show. To use the words of Rüdiger Folten, Head of Strategy and Design for Volkswagen AG, Wolfsburg, 'When we first started with Concept 1 it was only an idea. We initially wanted to produce a zero emission vehicle. VW sales were falling down in the U.S.A and so we wanted to do something which would make people remember we were still there.

Design rendition of Concept 1

We also wanted the shape to resemble something the American people remembered and were fond of, but it was also to be designed with modern style.' Concept 1 was scratch built and although many publications at the time thought it used the Polo platform, Rüdiger Folten assured that 'Concept 1 was without relation, it was not Polo or anything to do with Polo.'

Concept 1 was designed under top secret conditions at the VWOA Design Centre facility in Simi Valley, California, part of what Volkswagen AG refers to as its

North American Region. They were responsible for the project from start to finish.

Simi Valley was opened by Volkswagen and Audi in January 1991. The aim of the design centre was to improve the position of VW and Audi in the North American market. Volkswagen wanted to develop closer links with the market and to look into the trends of what is considered to be one of the hotbeds of automotive design.

In March 1992, work initially started at Simi Valley on a vehicle concept which relied on alternative power systems – the goal being zero emission. By September, VW had carried out extensive market research on the American automotive world and found that one thing kept coming up. When Volkswagen was mentioned, the instant reaction was the Beetle. It was a legendary car which remained strong in the memories of the American population. The Beetle was the synonym for VW right across North America.

Volkswagen realised it could act on the good feeling that the Beetle gave people, and in turn perhaps bring the VW name back into the limelight in the USA. The idea was given thought and the outcome was to combine the zero-emission study with a car which would revive the Beetle legend. This was not to be a simple retrospective design, even though the first impression would shout out Beetle! The curved roofline which slopes steeply at the back of the car, and the rounded bonnet in contour with the semicircular wings both indicate a strong link with the original Beetle, but at the same time

Similar lines with 48 years between them

Side view shows where the 'three circles' idea used on the New Beetle logo originated.

look new and refreshing.

By March 1993 the design had gone from artwork to three dimensional 1:4 scaled models, and Hartmut Warkuss, project initiator had met with VW Chief Executive Dr Ferdinand Piëch to present the study. The outcome of the meeting was very positive. Having seen the Concept 1 design study and obviously realising the potential high impact it could have on the automotive world, Dr. Piëch ordered for the study to be brought up to a full scale car, which would have to be ready to be debuted by VWOA at Detroit in January 1994.

The design team leader responsible for Concept 1, J.C.Mays – who has since moved to The Ford Motor Company – said 'We wanted to combine the past and the future.' The theory was to create a vehicle which everyone could immediately connect with, but one which also featured up to date technology. This was the foundation for the use of hybrid and electric engine ideas.

The design study brief was to give a choice of three power trains. First was the four cylinder 1.9 Litre/66kW Turbo Diesel with 5 speed Ecomatic transmission. For those unfamiliar with the Ecomatic it fundamentally consists of a computer controlled automatic shutdown system. If the computer decides the vehicle does not need the engine power at that moment, it simply switches the engine off. As the vehicle would pull up to a stop light the engine would cut out, and then as soon as the driver puts a foot on the accelerator pedal the engine would instantly fire-up again. Not only did this ingenious idea prove to be more fuel efficient, but it also cut emissions by 36 per cent. The Ecomatic initially feels strange to drive, but after an hour or so most people adjust. It certainly poses no problems for a confident driver. In Europe, VW offered the Ecomatic in the Golf, and although it was a worthwhile idea, the public in general didn't take to it. Within a year the Ecomatic was dropped. In Concept 1, the 1.9 TDI was capable of 180km/h (which equates to 111mp/h) and was able to go from 0-62mp/h in 12.8 seconds.

Secondly, the fully electric drive train which Concept 1 would theoretically offer was an AC Induction electric-powered two speed automatic which created 37kw of

The TDI engine with Ecomatic system

VW Concept 1 design renditions

power. This package, which relied on the AEG Sodium/Nickel Chloride high temperature battery, could propel Concept 1 to a top speed of 77.67 mp/h and give an urban range of just under 95 miles. Tests for constant speed range at 31 mp/h produced a range of 155 miles.

The third power train was a hybrid which consisted of a three cylinder 1400cc TDI which produced 50kW linked to the E-Motor, an AC Induction 18kw electric Nickel/Metalhydride powered unit. The diesel motor had a top speed of 102.5mp/h, while when switched over to electric power the maximum speed was 65.24mp/h.

By July 1993 the full scale clay mock-up of the Concept 1 was completed. It was a much smaller car than the production model New Beetle, the dimensions of which we will look at later. Initial comparisons highlight immediate differences between the original Beetle and Concept 1. The length of Concept 1 was 3824mm or 12.54 feet, which is in fact smaller in length than original rear-engined Beetle, which measured 13.35 feet. The width was 5.36 feet, wider than the original Beetle by 31 inches. An interesting point is that the original VW Beetle and Concept 1 are virtually the same height.

Preparation work continued to get the yellow show car ready in time for the show. The design

23

The interior of the Concept 1 show car

incorporated elements which harked back to the Beetle, but also many which were futuristic state-ments. To use VW's own words, 'The rounded forms have, wherever possible, been brought as close as possible to two basic geometrical shapes – the circle and the sphere. Smooth surfaces remain smooth, with no swage lines or ledges, deriving their subtle charm solely from their generous curves. The panel configuration is also logical and geometrically clear. There is a pleasing tension between the simplicity of the smooth surfaces and the few straight lines on the one hand, and the rounded shapes on the other – the lines of the side windows are a good example.'

When in silhouette or side view, Concept 1 would reveal something which was very different to the original Beetle. The windscreen was not upright! On Concept 1 the windscreen gave a smooth transi-tion from the front of the vehicle to the roof. This would give the driver and passengers a far more spacious feel and panoramic view. Anyone who has driven the original VW Beetle will tell you they felt very close to the upright windscreen.

The interior of the car was to feature black leather upholstery, muting the seats and highlighting the symmetrical layout of the very basic dashboard. The central air vent outlet/radio pod and large single display gauge were dark grey plastic, whilst co-ordinated yellow sections to the left and right made the dashboard blend in with the doors. The passenger's side of the dashboard featured a large grab handle, with a flower vase to its left. This was a simple trick to tie in with the original Beetle, as glass or china dash mounted flower vases were very popular during the fifties and early sixties. However, although very popular, they were not a standard Beetle feature, and were only offered as accessories. Be this as it may, this simple idea gained a huge amount of press coverage for VW, and made it into production on the New Beetle!

Running from the bulkhead under the dash between the front seats and through to the rear seat, Concept 1 had a colour coded yellow tunnel cover which incorporated two beverage cup holders in front of the transmission shifter, along with a further cup holder in the rear. Both of the inner door sills were also colour coded. Both interior door panels were basic, featuring simple door pulls, winder handles and door lock pulls. The inner door tops were colour coded as well, and this theme carried on through to the underside of the rear quarter windows.

On the outside

Moving out of the cockpit, the concept car was equipped with very large 18 inch six-spoked wheels with 155/75 Goodyear tires. The width of the tires helped give the impression that they were tall and skinny, and therefore similar to the original Beetle. Exterior details included two Beetle styled horn-grilles. A direct link was present with the aluminium grilles found on the front wings/fenders of the original VW Beetle. One of these had the horn behind it, but the other was just blanked off – there for reasons of symmetry. These did not make it into production.

The bonnet/hood of Concept 1 was shorter and less bulbous than later production models, giving the vehicle a much more curved shape in profile than the production car. The headlights incorporated the front turn signals. The front also featured what would appear to be a removable lower front panel or apron, which was designed to be changed as per the registration or licence plate requirements of different markets. The apron also featured small high power mini spot lights.

All four wings or fenders were designed to be interchangeable from corner to corner. For example, one front fender could be swapped for the opposite rear fender and vice-versa. This was a fantastic idea which would have halved dealer panel stocks and orders, but unfortunately it proved impractical in series production. The rear bumper was smooth and followed the curve of the wing/fender, assisting with the three curve profile of the vehicle. Again this would be lost in production. As with the front bumper, the rear featured a separate apron, but rather than having lights, the rear apron had an exhaust tail pipe cut out and, on the opposite side, a towing hook. Moving to the boot lid, Concept 1 was equipped with a third brake light, VW roundel and boot lock.

At this stage we should consider the feelings of the VW enthusiasts (or should that be zealots?), as part of the design of Concept 1 was to move away from the rear mounted air-cooled engine linked to a swing axle or independent rear suspension transmission. The new car had a front mounted engine and transmission and was to be front wheel drive. This was a large departure which made many feel that although the car might look like a Beetle, it would never be a real Beetle. The Beetle design had not really been changed since 1977 except for updates and improvements. However, if the model had remained the mainstay of Volkswagen sales in Europe and America, it could well have progressed to the front engine/front wheel drive layout. As it was dropped from the European and American markets by the Golf and its derivatives, and only produced for South American markets, we will never know what might have happened to the Beetle and its layout.

The basic flight deck of Concept 1

What we do know is that the story was about to become even more exciting, as Concept 1 was ready to go public at the Detroit Auto Show. VW admitted the response exceeded all expectations. The car created enormous interest. Of course part of the reason was the obvious association with its predecessor. The attention to detail and quality in the design was also obvious.

At the launch, Ulrich Seiffert, VW's Executive Director of Technology and Development, told the press, 'The intention is to emphasise the typical qualities of a VW; its honest, reliable, timeless and youthful design. We will never bring the Beetle back, but we would like to go back to our roots with

an honest, reliable car. It will influence the design of our smaller product range.'

At this stage there was no statement made about the possibility of putting Concept 1 into production, mainly because VW hadn't made any plans to do so! However, the reaction from the public, press and VW dealers all across North America was extremely positive. Everybody seemed to want VW to build this car! Volkswagen clearly had to start thinking very seriously about taking steps to put the vehicle into production. When the press asked Steiffert if VW would put the Concept 1 into production, his first, rather muted reaction was that it was 'possible'. The most important question at VW was, as Rüdiger Folten puts it 'will we be able to take this shape, which is well known, and make it work?'

The next step was to unveil a further study on the Concept 1 theme, the Concept 1 Cabriolet. The success at Detroit was continued at the Geneva Motor Show. If going back to its roots worked so well for VW with the sedan, there was little doubt over whether or not a Cabriolet version would create a

The Concept 1 cabriolet – the logical progression

stir. The prototype was heralded as a glimpse into the future of Volkswagen, a car which was in a class of its own, simple, unique and modern, looking forward optimistically but still showing its heritage.

It was at this stage that Dr Piëch promised the motoring world that Concept 1 'need not remain just a vision.' A press release from Wolfsburg followed shortly after and stated: 'Volkswagen AG Approves Concept 1. Wolfsburg, Germany – Volkswagen's popular Concept 1 automobile, a design study car that created a public and media sensation upon its unveiling at the 1994 North American International Auto Show in Detroit, Michigan, will be produced and on the market before the year 2000, Volkswagen confirmed. The Volkswagen AG Board of Management gave its approval in November 1994 for the development of Concept 1. The decision came in response to appeals from enthusiasts all over the world who embraced the design concept. Volkswagen said the United States will be one of the primary markets for the new car.'

VW later said the economic production and marketable pricing would only be possible on the basis of what Volkswagen call a platform. In addition, it was decided to base the production vehicle on what Rüdiger Folten referred to as the 'future Golf, which later became "Golf 4."' For this to become reality, Concept 1 would need to go through many changes. But as Folten humorously said, 'When Dr. Piëch says we will produce this car, 7,000 people go to work.'

But the Concept 1 wasn't finished with yet. The Cabriolet version was shown in the U.S. at the New York Auto Show. At that time, VW told us, 'the Concept 1 Cabriolet embodies the spirit of Volkswagen with the flair of open air motoring. From the original people's car to people's cars, Volkswagen has continued its motoring evolution. Dependable, reliable, well engineered. Today, Concept 1 and Concept 1 Cabriolet capture the future ideas of what a Volkswagen could be. The growth of the fourth largest auto manufacturer in the world continues with a keen look at future driving needs – needs that blend the heritage of the company with advanced technology.'

The Volkswagen design team in the United States set out to design a car that brought together the past and future. It was to be a grand design, a car that people could relate to and put their trust in, whilst it still offered them the impact of advanced technology. The Concept 1 and Concept 1 Cabriolet were the results of that effort. In profile the car has

Concept 1 Cabriolet in side profile. Fabulous!

VW, you simply have to build a New Beetle Cabriolet!

a clean, simple shape. It is formed from three cylinders – two where the wheels are positioned, and one forming the passenger cabin. There are no aggressive lines.

The car was designed with the motor up front, dual airbags, side impact beams and ABS brakes, and it seated four adults. The 18inch tires were 155/75. All interior lighting on the instrument panel was electroluminescent, which goes a long way to help lessen eye strain. Driver information came from a single round gauge that encompassed the speedometer, engine temperature indicator, fuel gauge, and headlight switch. The Concept 1 Cabriolet also included an AM/FM stereo and a compact disc player with six speakers. Furthermore, the seats and side panels featured impressively stylish woven black and white cloth inlays.

There can be no doubt in the matter – it was the stunning design of Concept 1 which provided the impetus that drove VW to put the New Beetle into construction.

3

Design & Manufacture

The story now moves away from Simi Valley to the design studios of Wolfsburg in Germany, where the task of turning the motor show concept into a tangible production vehicle settled. At a glance, Concept 1 may appear very similar to the production models of the New Beetle, but when you actually compare the two, little remained unchanged. The 'future Golf' platform was virtually a foot longer than the overall length of Concept 1. As Rüdiger Folten, puts it 'The car needed to be bigger – larger, higher, longer – so we had to make it to grow a little.'

Design rendition of the New Beetle

The Wolfsburg team set about re-designing, starting with renditions and then moving onto computer designs. Then a platform was set up as a base for a full size clay model which was worked from a industrial plasticine mass to the required shape by hand using scrapers, modelling tools and templates. Once the design was finalised, further models, firstly without windows and later with them, were produced by casting a substance known as Epowood, which is actually a form of plastic.

Next the Epowood presentation model was measured with a data probe to form the basis for the first prototypes. The data was then programmed into computers and digitised, to be used for the man-

Early design drawings retained Concept 1 mirrors

ufacture of bodywork tooling. Typically, this data also assists with further studies into detail, such as crash simulations and other intricate tests.

The next step was to move onto the interior of the car. The technical design team had to create the internal elements of the body, including load-bearing structures, reinforcements, pillars, sills and inner wings, along with components such as the dashboard, door and lid hinges, interior door panels and bulkhead. To give you an idea of the amount of work involved, the body of a Volkswagen consists of around 300 stamped or pressed steel panels, all of which must pass stringent testing for quality and safety, along with being economically viable to produce!

Interior design was equally important. The inside had to be appealing. After all, this is the part of the car which the driver and passengers see the most of. Visually, the vehicle was ergonomically designed to be 'perfect.' Apart from being designed with up to the minute safety features, the functions had to be 'self explanatory.' In short, this was a very hard task for those concerned. In the same way that the exterior evolved, the interior started with the Concept 1 idea, from which further artists renditions were drawn, and then a full scale wood and plasticine model of the interior – which VW refers to as the 'seat box' – was built. The seat box is where small details and functions are designed.

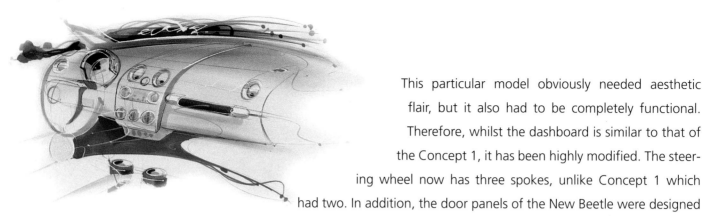

Dashboard design renditions

This particular model obviously needed aesthetic flair, but it also had to be completely functional. Therefore, whilst the dashboard is similar to that of the Concept 1, it has been highly modified. The steering wheel now has three spokes, unlike Concept 1 which had two. In addition, the door panels of the New Beetle were designed to incorporate netted door pockets, moulded armrests and door pulls, and were given the added safety feature of a red warning light which illuminates when the door is open. When attending to the layout of the engine and drive train the Wolfsburg Design team also had to take into account the things we take for granted, such as checking the oil and windscreen washer levels.

The Colour and Trim Department were the next team to work on the project. Working from a virtually infinite choice, they had to work out which colours this car would available in, taking into account current trends and attempting to offer a colour which should meet every customer's needs. Eight colours were chosen for the production vehicle. The interior materials, colours and finishes were all carefully chosen to be harmonious with not only the exterior finishes, but also each other. The Design and Trim Department is like a Paris fashion house, as it must not only meet with the customer's needs, but also come up with new and exciting trim ideas and trends.The first full scale exterior and interior models were presented to the Volkswagen Board of Management in November 1994 for approval.

A new beginning

The next stage should actually be seen as 'a new chapter in the New Beetle story,' says Folten. A sheet metal concept car was built with the aim of unveiling the model in October 1995 at the Tokyo Motor Show, the first showing of Concept 1 or its derivatives in Asia. Although Rüdiger Folten stresses 'there were no secrets about the new Beetle,' not much had been said since March 1994. This made the press sceptical that VW would be able to keep the attraction of Concept 1 during the transition from show car to production vehicle. VW dispelled that rumour decisively at Tokyo with the black prototype car!

Volkswagen had to make comprehensive changes at the front end of the vehicle, mainly for

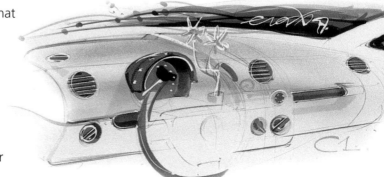

safety reasons, but managed to keep it as close as possible to the lines of Concept 1. At this stage the car was known simply as Concept, and had a full tinted glass roof, which worked very well with the black paint work. What the media did not know when they came away from Tokyo was that the black Concept car was, as Rüdiger Folten states, 'very close to the final production model.' The Japanese public gave the Concept a truly amazing reception, with an astonishing 20,000 advance orders placed at the show. VW were on to a winner. The positive stream of enthusiasm from VW dealers, the media and prospective buyers had paid off.

Dr Piëch told the world it would produce the Concept car before the millennium. He also announced that Volkswagen was to produce the vehicle at its North American production facility at Puebla, Mexico. Further more, Puebla would produce the vehicle not only to serve the needs of the North American market, but for markets world-wide. On the 29th of October 1995, VW issued a press release which was entitled 'Volkswagen announces production site for Concept 1.' It contained some

The VW Concept, built for Tokyo, was close to the later production model

Little was changed at this stage

of Dr Piëch's written remarks released at the Tokyo Motor Show press conference. He said, 'You will undoubtedly be aware that we are currently in the process, and I say process advisedly because it is an ongoing thing, of developing the Concept 1. Naturally we are doing this with the most advanced technologies. However, instead of keeping the car under wraps up to the time of its launch we want our customers to participate in the product development of the Concept 1. We invite you to take an active role. This exemplifies the customer orientation of the Volkswagen Group.

'When we first presented Concept 1 at the 1994 Detroit Motor Show, we were overwhelmed by the positive response. Since then we have talked to customers and dealers all over the world, and taken careful note of the recommendations of the media and motoring press. Why? Because we want to put a car on the markets of the world that perfectly corresponds to the requirements, the desires and dreams of our customers.Today we invite you to acquaint yourselves with the current status of Concept 1. Look at the car, and when doing so, please bear in mind that the memories of yesteryear can also form the basis for the dreams of tomorrow. Concept 1 embodies a vision that redefines the memories of yesteryear.

'As a proof of our confidence in the Concept 1, we are today announcing the scheduled production location for this car: the Concept 1 will be built for all markets at our Puebla factory in Mexico. This will strengthen the consistent endeavour of the Volkswagen Group to deploy global presence and to create enthusiasm among customers with our products.'

The New Beetle appears

The Mexican factory certainly made the most sense, as the main target market for the new model was just over the border, rather than across an ocean! The tax situation would also be better for customers based within the United States as the car would not be an import from Europe.

Five months after the production news, VW was back at the Geneva Motor Show and the car was officially named the 'New Beetle.' Volkswagen had honed the Concept design and

The start of production in Mexico

At the end of the production line

as Rüdiger Folten told us, 'this was, apart from detail changes, the final stage of development.' An interesting feature of the Geneva New Beetle prototype was the drive train, which was a TDI engine linked to four wheel drive. The vehicle again met with a positive reception from all sides.

The interior of the Geneva New Beetle had a grey-yellow combination of fabric and leather, which gave an impression of lightness. The fuel tank capacity was 55 litres, which combined with the 90bhp TDI engine to give a highly respectable driving range before further fuel had to be added. Drag coefficient was also mentioned for the first time at Geneva, and despite the unmistakably unique shape, the drag coefficient was well below the critically sought-after 40 mark.

Now it was just a simple case of producing the car. That wasn't entirely straight-forward, as Volkswagen had to build an entirely new production line alongside the original Beetle production line at Puebla. Build quality to European standards had to be assured, and the factory needed to be able to cope with a rise in production. The Volkswagen Group plans to have released somewhere in the range of 100,000 – 160,000 units by the end of the year 2000. Each car leaving the factory wears a small decal in each door window which states 'Proudly Produced With High Quality Volkswagen de Mexico.' The car wears its production heritage proudly, in full view.

New Beetles at the Puebla factory gate

4

Launch, Hype & Sales

'Reborn January 5, 1998' was the single line statement from the cover of the New Beetle

brochure at the launch of the model at the Detroit Auto Show. The VW press release said of

the New Beetle, 'The engine's in the front, but its heart's in the same place.' Seven New

Beetles were on display at Detroit, and the atmosphere was said to have been 'electric.' The

hot news was that the car was set to arrive in the spring of 1998 'at Volkswagen dealers

across America.' The New Beetle proves that something very good in a past life can come

back as something even better, something totally new.

**The engine's in the front,
but its heart's in the same place.**

One of the many witty VW postcards

While it rekindles the magic of its legendary namesake, the New Beetle is not an update of the original but a completely new and modern car – a Beetle driving forward into the 21st century, optimistically inviting us to follow. As a contemporary creation, the New Beetle is more than a ray of sunny originality in an all-too-serious car market. It is also fully functional, with plenty of creature comforts and the very latest advancements in small-car safety.

It is significantly larger than the original, both inside and out, and shares no parts with its predecessor. It is pow-

This cut-away shows the heart of the Golf 4...

ered by a front mounted 115 horsepower four cylinder engine or, optionally, a highly advanced Turbo direct-injection diesel that delivers an EPA rating of 48 miles per gallon on the highway and a driving range of nearly 700 miles.

The New Beetle uses front wheel drive and is equipped with a wealth of standard items, including CFC-free air conditioning, a pollen and odour filter, a six speaker stereo with CD-control capability, beverage holders, an anti-theft alarm, halogen projector-beam headlights, four wheel disc brakes and central locking system with remote. It can be ordered with a further wealth of extras, including electronic ABS brakes, alloy wheels, cruise control, leather seating, integrated fog lamps, heatable front seats, and one touch up and down power windows.

As a priority in its development, the New Beetle's advanced occupant safety system includes energy absorbing crush zones, pre-tensioning front seat belts, front and rear headrests, daytime running lights, dual airbags and front seat-mounted side air bags.

This New Beetle was autographed at the Los Angeles launch

Based on Volkswagen's new Golf chassis – Europe's number-one selling car – the New Beetle is built to the highest standards. This is clearly expressed in its solid, one piece appearance, which results from narrow panel gap tolerances in production. By using state-of-the-art production techniques like laser welding, Volkswagen has given the New Beetle unmatched torsional and body rigidity. Its fully galvanised body allows for a 12-year warranty against corrosion or rust perforation.

Clive Warrilow, President and CEO, Volkswagen of America Inc, said, 'Some may have predicted a retro car, but as you can see, the New Beetle is a completely modern design, almost futuristic. It is designed to appeal to people who fondly recall the past, as well as young people who have no connection at all to the original. Where the original provided basic transportation, the New Beetle is an upmarket, lifestyle vehicle. It's highly emotional, a car that makes the experience of driving fun again.'

Volkswagen of America Inc. handed out 1000 special Press Packs at Detroit. These were held in black cloth bags with the New Beetle logo on the front. Inside, along with a press release, photographs and slide, there was a Compact Disc entitled 'Dream the same Dream,' which contained the music used at the launch, and a plastic bud vase, just like the one fitted to the dashboard of the New Beetle. This came with its own logo-embossed metal stand.

On the same day as the New Beetle was launched at Cobo Hall, Detroit, Volkswagen launched the car in Los Angeles California at the L.A. Auto Show. Part of the launch involved a card game that all visitors could enter. Winners were given the opportunity to sign their name on the paintwork of the black Beetle on display with a special white pen, and the signed car was later sent to a VW museum. There was also a chance to race on a four-lane VW Golf slot car track. Heat winners were photographed sitting in a red New Beetle on display, and the photograph was then mounted in a Beetle-shaped frame. The whole launch was meant to be fun for all.

The New Beetle lured all types of people to the stand and everyone was excited. People came from different generations and from a diverse range of occupations, but all were enthusiastic about the New Beetle. One particular long term VW enthusiast called Blue Nelson from Marina Del Rey, California,

On show to the public for the first time!

January 9th, 1998 – the Vancouver New Beetle launch

heard that the Canadian New Beetle launch was to be held in Vancouver, British Columbia four days later, on the 9th of January. He immediately dropped everything and booked a flight to Vancouver. His association with the New Beetle didn't stop at being one of the only enthusiasts to visit two launches, but you will find out more later.

The Volkswagen Canada Inc. stand consisted of a revolving display with a metallic blue New Beetle, but as with the L.A. stand it was hard to get up close to the car due to the sheer number of people surrounding it. A second car was on the floor and was open for the public to get inside and examine – the only problem was that the queue was very long! The same enthusiastic buzz which had been witnessed at Detroit was present at both L.A. and Vancouver. Over-worked sales representatives were on hand to take orders and deposits. After the four years of media hype since Detroit 1994, the launch of the New Beetle was about to become the best publicity the company could have wished for. The press went absolutely ballistic!

The New Beetle was in the news in every conceivable format. The car was covered in numerous motoring magazines, in local and national tabloid newspapers and on the regional, national and international television. In Britain, the launch of New Beetle was given a piece on the major Independent Television News programme *News at Ten*. This proves its magnitude, as it is difficult to recall another Volkswagen making it onto this programme. The New Beetle must also go down in history as one of the first cars – if not the very first – to have its launch covered across the Internet.

New Beetles would continue to be in the news throughout the year but media coverage was only the tip of the iceberg. Public interest, which had always been high, was about to step up a gear, and it is doubtful whether VW was ready for the New Beetle-mania which was about to break out. The response to this car became overwhelming and in some cases very emotional. America wanted to buy the car, straight away. The race was on to be the first to own one, the first in the country, the first in the area, the first in the town, the first in the street. Of course some astute people had already got their names down, while others had to find a VW dealer who hadn't already got a huge waiting list. Most dealers had a minimum of 50 or 60 orders, and many had far more. Some were into the hundreds and figured that the waiting list could be as long as a year and a half!

The first retail releases

The New Beetle was basically designed for the American market, and so America was the first to receive the car. VW said it would start to see the first batch of around 4,000 cars delivered to the 599 dealers in the North American network towards the end of March. The rest of the world would not see the car on sale for at least another six months. Many of those in the long line of customers wishing to buy the New Beetle were willing to pay over and above the listed 'sticker' price to have the privilege of being one of the first to be seen in this much talked about VW.

The base 'suggested retail price' from Volkswagen for a standard 2.0 litre was listed at $15,200. The diesel was listed at $16,475, but on top of both prices a destination charge of $500 was to be added. Then there were taxes, dealer charges, registration charges and any optional extras to be added.

All the cars in the first batch to be delivered were equipped with the optional $410 Sports Package. This consisted of projector beam fog lights and alloy wheels, along with the Convenience Packs, which gave power windows and cruise control. So the average 'sticker' price of the first batch of cars was around $17,000. However, as soon as the first batch

Clive Warrilow, President of VWOA, at Detroit

The New Beetle press pack is already collectable!

were driven out of the dealerships, New Beetle owners were being stopped in the street and offered an instant profit if they would sell the car. In some cases, this inducement was as much as $10,000!

America had gone mad about the New Beetle. If a VW dealer had an unsold car in the showroom, prospective buyers were bidding against each other for the cars. In many cases the sales staff either sat back and watched the prices rise and rise until one of the bidders gave up, or became referees and broke up the ensuing squabble! One rumour was that two people were arguing over the price of a car for so long that a third person came in and bought the car from another salesman. At other dealerships the customers were getting so heated that they had to be escorted off the premises. Some people wanted a Beetle so much that they followed delivery transporters to dealerships.

Demand causes problems

As with anything which is in demand, there are always a few shrewd business people out there who can smell a profit. So it wasn't long before New Beetles were being sold through non-franchised dealers at marked-up prices. The Internet came into play, and advertisements for 'turn key' cars for $20,000 plus started to appear. Of course, by buying one these cars you get an auto quickly, but there is every likelihood you may find you have lost the 100,000 mile/10 year warranty.

While many of the VW dealers made hay while the sun was shining, commanding even more than $20,000 for New Beetles, Volkswagen of America were powerless to do anything about the mania. Of course, when production really gets going it might be possible to walk into a VW dealership and buy a car in the desired colour for the 'sticker price,' but this day could be a while away yet.

Meanwhile, those who were amongst the first to own the New Beetle – such as Jeff Grewing from Sacramento, Randy Carlson from Brea, California, Bill Kessler from Detroit, Pamela Brown from Cleveland, James Howard from Kansas City, Brian Burrows and Luke Theochari from London, England and Romano Schmidt from Germany – can soak up the envious and admiring looks of every other road user while they quite literally stop traffic in their New Beetles.

When it came to advertising the New Beetle, Volkswagen took a very 'tongue in cheek' route. As with the original campaigns of Doyle Dayne and Bernbach, Volkswagen of America went for simple statements to get the point across. One such advert read 'Nought to 60? Yes!' Another interesting approach was simply to have the text line 'What colour do you dream in?' or 'One for each day of the week' alongside a photograph of a New Beetle in every available colour. Other nice lines were 'Less flower more power,' 'A work of art with side impact airbags... and a bud vase,' and 'The engine's in the front, but its heart's in the same place.'

In a way, VW doesn't need to do too much in the way of promotion. The media has more or less taken care of that for them. In fact, VW itself took care of the advertising when it designed the car, as every New Beetle on the street is advertising. VW has created something unique and instantly recognisable, unlike most other new models, which look very similar to the rest of the pack. Have you recently found yourself wondering what a new car is and then got a surprise when you got close enough to see the badge on the back? There is not much chance of that happening with the New Beetle – just like the original.

This VW postcard tells it like it is!

A positive form of ID.

The New Beetle was introduced to Europe's press at Volkswagen's headquarters at the Wolfsburg factory between the 2nd and 6th of November 1998, and only a fortunate few were invited to this unique launch. VW flew journalists to Hanover airport, and then laid on a fleet of VW buses to ferry them to Wolfsburg. After a German buffet lunch in the management restaurant, we were able to take either a 1.9TDi or 2.0Litre Euro model for a 45 minute test drive.

The Euro Beetle differs in many ways from the U.S. model, mostly to meet the different regulations. For instance, the headlights have side lights, and the running lights/turn signals are simply turn signals. Further, each Euro Beetle is also fitted with side-mounted turn signal indicators set in the quater panel on each side, under the rear view mirrors. The rear bumper has been re-designed to accept the longer, thinner licence plates used in many European countries and is missing the running lights at each corner. One of the back-up/reversing lights has been changed to a fog light. One particularly appealing feature is the new badging – both the front and rear badges have become chrome bases with white enamel VW logoes on a dark blue enamel background.

Following on from the US '99 model, VW also announced that a glass tilting/sliding sunroof is now an optional extra. Further options included cruise control and a VW accessory roof rack. Two new body colours were also announced, Lemon Yellow and Cameo Blue, both solid pastel colours. The European models were distributed from November 1998 onwards.

Perhaps the most noteworthy addition announced for the European model was ESP, or the Electronic Stability Program. This is a system which 'reliably suppresses unwanted under- or oversteer when close to the handling limits.' However, the most exciting news came as a quote in the VW Press Pack – 'An additional power unit is also planned for introduction in the course of the coming year (1999): a 110kW, 150bhp V5 with a displacement of 2.3 Litres is to be the new top engine option.'

After an evening presentation by the VW Board, VW laid on the most memorable launch party ever. This fantastic sixties-themed stage show included songs from the musical "Hair," a Beatles tribute band and a German lady emulating Janis Joplin. The launch was an experience I will never forget.

5

On the Road

Cars are not produced simply to be talked about, they exist to be driven and to get you

to your destination as safely as possible. However, we all like something with a bit of style

and charisma, and on the road the New Beetle gives the driver an experience very few cars

can provide – the sensation of being on the receiving end of virtually undivided attention from

most of the people around you, both pedestrians and other road users.

Phenomenal head-turner!

There are not many cars which will turn heads in the way the New Beetle does. In fact, it creates such a stir that it can be unnerving at times. Have you ever driven through a built up area such as a town and actually had people pointing at you, waving at you, clapping their hands and shouting at you? Well if you have, then the chances are that you are either a famous celebrity, or you are driving a New Beetle. This car really does cause a commotion. You will genuinely see people in the street pointing at the car, and if you have the windows down you can hear them saying 'Look, that's the New Beetle.' Even with the windows shut, you can often read their lips. Personally speaking, I have never witnessed this phenomenon behind the wheel of any other car. If you don't like a lot of attention, or suffer from paranoia, then the New Beetle is certainly not the car for you – at least, not for a few years yet!

Out on the open road, the New Beetle is a pleasure to drive

In traffic, other drivers ask questions, or honk their horns, or simply smile and give you the thumbs up. When you stop for fuel, the attendants ask how it drives and whether you like it. If you stop any-where, you will be greeted like an old friend by people who want to look at this new car. Complete strangers will come up to you and tell you how they used to have a Beetle, and how much they loved it. Others will actually try to get you to take them for a ride in the car.

The weirdest thing is that we are talking about people from all walks of life and age groups. It does-n't seem to matter if it is a student, a business person, a retired couple, a young parent – whoever they are, they seem to know exactly what this car is. Now this could be put down to the high profile media coverage, but it is doubtful every admiring glance is due to good press. From the minute you first set eyes on the New Beetle, you know what it is – it's the New Beetle, it can't be anything else. The Volkswagen master plan has paid off stunningly!

Metallic paint finishes make the New Beetle look even more chic

However, it is when people get a close look at the New Beetle that things become really interesting. Many find the car is 'far bigger' than they expected. Most feel it's pretty or cute; in my experience, only a few people thought it was ugly! On sitting inside the first thing that most people comment on is the dashboard. As they lean forward and touch it, the comments are generally 'this looks really big!', or 'Wow! This dash is huge!' Next it seems to be the headroom, touching the headliner and saying 'This is high up' and 'You could wear a top hat in here.'

One area which does seem to create negative feelings is the plastic roof liner which runs down the

Build quality is, in general, high

'C' post in each of the rear corners: 'I don't like this, this feels weird on the side of my head.' The most prominent negative factor however was the capping on the door and rear window, which was an unpopular shade of red. The turbo-charged 1.8T has optional GLX trim to replace the standard New Beetle's GLS, including six-spoke alloy wheels, a great speed-activated rear spoiler, leather seating, and much more besides.

The predominant feeling towards the New Beetle is definitely positive. In virtually every case, people didn't just look at the vehicle, the felt that they had to touch it. It was as though they were meeting up with an old friend.

First impressions

When given the keys to the New Beetle, you find out its good and bad points very quickly. Firstly, when walking around the car, the lines, tight gaps and smooth exterior features, such as the way the headlights and taillights are flush fitted, are appealing to the eye. The slightly different hue or tone of the colour of the nearly-matched door mirrors is the only let-down from the outside. Getting into the car proves to be the second disappointment, for those used to central locking. The remote electronic key – which can sound the horn in the form of a panic system, set the alarm and lock both doors – has one drawback; it doesn't open the passenger door! To open the passenger door you need to either 'unlock' the driver's door twice with the normal key or use the remote to open the driver's door and then reach in and press the electric central locking switch. Both options offer little comfort to a passenger standing in the rain! The rear hatch can be opened via a very nice little switch which boasts a New Beetle logo, located on the driver's door, or from the outside of the car by rotating the VW roundel to expose the keyhold for the boot lock and using the ignition key to unlock it.

Once inside the New Beetle and behind the steering wheel for the first time you notice something – the dashboard! It is huge. The driver can not reach the windscreen. In fact it is doubtful that an orang-utan could! The dash looks very interesting though. Initially one could be tricked into thinking they were about to set off on a mission in a spacecraft of some kind, rather than a drive in a car. The materials used in the dashboard, especially those in the pronounced centre section – which houses the

Note how different this model looks without fog lights

stereo, two ventilation outlets and various controls – do not look or feel very good. This is quite sad, as the dash is the part of the car the driver sees the most. Personally speaking, I think that VW could have gone for something which looked a little more sporty and expensive, such as carbon fibre, and made the dash into a truly impressive feature.

The feel of the steering wheel and the passenger grab handle are satisfying, even thought they are made from the same composite material. Behind the steering wheel and in front of the passenger are two areas at the front of the dash which have a rough finish plastic and look great. Beyond these you find more tacky smooth plastic, which for some reason is flat. The opinion of many people is that this could easily have been a great area for trinket storage, although you'd have to stretch a long way to retrieve anything. Instead it is a sun trap, and on a fine sunny day it creates quite bad reflection on the windscreen, which can be trying. There is a spot for eyeglasses on the '99 rear view mirror, though.

You can not help but like the single instrument binnacle which incorporates the speedometer, fuel gauge, tachometer and mileage/trip read out. It is functional without being hard to read in any way. The binnacle also provides warning lights which let you know whether the lights are on, the indicators are flashing, the trunk is open and so on. For '99, the clock is well-placed below the rear view mirror.

The much talked-about flower vase and the area it sits do not, sadly, meet expectations. Again,

they look a bit cheap. The stereo, however, is great, both in design and performance – easy to get the hang of and not tricky to use. Ergonomically speaking, it is a success. All three ventilation controls are simple to operate, as are the air-conditioning and re-circulation switches. The only hope is that air-conditioning is not dropped from the standard specification on certain markets, as demisting the windscreen quickly and safely is made very much easier by good air-conditioning.

Moving to the doors, and without dwelling on the unfortunate door cappings, the controls are again very straightforward. The electronic mirror controls are situated in the capping, in front of the door locking switch and the door handle, which is chromed. Below this you find the door panel itself which blends in nicely with the lines of the dashboard. The door panel on the driver's side houses the fuel filler release and trunk release switches, electric window switches or window winder handle. Below these you will find the netted storage bins, which are large enough for a cellular phone, your favourite cassette and a packet of cigarettes, although the standard is to have no ashtray. In the '99 model, a handy joystick allows you to adjust the wing mirrors.

Settling in

The column mounted switches which control the indicators and wipers are simple to use, as are the main light switch and dash dimmer switch. Many of these components were found to have been made by Volkswagen's German suppliers, and the seat belts were made in Austria.

Both front seats offer the driver and passenger a great range of positions. By the side of each seat

is a lever which will bring the height of the seat up or down. The backrest can also be adjusted, as can the reach of the seat. With a little work the ideal driving position can be found, especially as the steering column offers reach and height adjustments. The headrests work too, particularly the '99 ring versions. You can actually rest your head on them when driving.

Rear seat space is adequate, even for a six footer, although occasional adult use for short journeys is probably the best bet. Children will have no problems in the back of the New Beetle. The rear seat can also folded be to provide extra luggage space, although for design reasons the width of entry to the trunk is limited. The rear seats also feature reading lights in the '99 model, which is a great touch for any book-loving passenger.

Between the seats, the central console features three cup holders. These are fixed and cannot be removed for cleaning. The material used is again fairly cheap looking. The sturdy hand-brake lever has a good grip and features a large chrome button. The lever recesses into the console, rather than standing proud.

In motion

Driving the New Beetle is a super experience even without the "Wow!" factor of being seen in it. However, you can't start the car unless the clutch pedal is depressed! In 2.0 litre, 115bhp form it isn't particularly fast, but the 1.8 litre turbocharged version yields an exciting 150bhp. The car is very quiet, in terms of both mechanical and wind noise. The suspension is comfortable without being too comfortable and the handling is good when tight corners come into play.

However, tight corners can be a problem as a blind spot is created by the 'A' pillars and the

Stunning car, stunning skyline!

exterior mirrors, which are mounted quite high up on the car. This obstruction can not be overcome, and is something you have to come to terms with. The design of the car also requires the driver to become accustomed to the large rear 'C' pillars for the same reason. Whilst diagonal views may be slightly impaired, the front, rear and side views are very good. New Beetle drivers may find it tricky to get used to the fact the windscreen is further away and what lies ahead of it is an unknown quantity – the furthest forward component in view being the windscreen wipers. It can be hard to work out how wide the car is and where the front bumper is. Parking is therefore best accomplished with a certain degree of careful consideration.

The car is very comfortable, and even after a 300 mile journey there is little, if any feeling of fatigue. A few have said the seats are too firm, but many others have found this not to be the case. One of the first questions about the New Beetle was whether or not it would be skittish and wander over the road in cross winds, like the original. The answer to both questions is no. The car drives with the same easy competence as the Golf it shares its running gear with. Even at speeds over 100mph (160kmh) – reached purely for research purposes on private ground of course – on long sweeping roads with a good side wind, the New Beetle felt completely safe. It must be said that the tail end of the car did feel lighter at high speed, but this was certainly not unnerving in anyway. Fortunately, the brakes are very good, with discs all on all four wheels – all ABS in the '99 model. Most importantly, the stopping power is certainly as good as the average motorist will ever need, even in an emergency stopping situation.

For many owners the New Beetle becomes more exciting to drive at night, and this is due to the fantastic dash illumination. The first time the dash is seen at night the comment is usually 'Wow!' The speedo binnacle lights up in a sort of neon blue, along with the readout on the cassette. The speedo

The car to be seen in around town

It will soon be time to switch the lights on – good news for the driver!

and gauge needle glow red, as do all the cassette, ventilation and other controls. This not only looks truly superb but is also very easy to drive with. There is no eye strain or fatigue associated with this feature, just a whole load of style and charisma.

On top of the basic price of the New Beetle, there are a number of alternatives which will offer higher performance, greater luggage capacity and extra internal space, but try to select those which don't disappear into irrelevancy once you're out on the open road. The bottom line is that it is the car that makes the difference, not the accessories that go with it. If you want to stand out from the crowd, you want a New Beetle. It's as simple as that.

6

Options

Virtually as soon as the New Beetle was in the hands of the public, the race was on to modify the cars. This phenomenon has been part of the original VW Beetle scene for decades, but there are two very separate areas of modification to consider. The first centres on performance, and the second caters for those who prefer classic vintage VWs.

From the start, after-market companies made every kind of accessory you could think of to spice up the basic specification of the old Beetle. One such item was the bud vase, which is part of the standard specification of the new version. During the fifties German companies such as Rosenthall offered porcelain vases for the original Beetle which were very popular. Today, many vintage Beetle enthusiasts will pay dearly for an original Rosenthall vase, rather than settle for a cheaper reproduction. Other

Randy Carlson's New Beetle on CEC alloys

items offered for Beetles in days gone by included slatted wooden roof racks, which again are in big demand and available as reproductions. A company based in Utah, called 'Parts', already offers a slatted wooden roof rack for the New Beetle. Many more original Beetle-style options are on their way.

The performance after-market for the New Beetle is also big business, and from the way things are going, it's certainly going to grow. Randy Carlson has to get the credit for being first out of the starting blocks. He picked up his metallic blue New Beetle and started to modify it straight

McKenna's flamed Beetle – the first custom paint job

away. The car was soon seen wearing a set of CEC 18 x 8.25 inch alloy wheels with 235/40 18 Pirelli P7000 tires, sitting on 1.25 inch lower upgraded springs by Eibach. The suspension was also beefed up with upgraded sway-bars. The standard exhaust tail pipe was changed for a Remus unit. Since then a number of other little tricks have been added to the car, and there are no signs of him stopping yet. Randy has since started the New Beetle club, which is based in California and is already very popular. If you are fortunate enough to own one, you can see his details – along with other interesting con-tacts – in the data section at the end of this book.

A Volkswagen dealership in Huntington Beach, California, called McKennas VW, was next to join in the fun with a Hot Rod styled New Beetle. McKennas took a black car to a local custom paint spe-cialist where it was given a fifties-styled flamed paint job from the front fenders to the rear of the doors. The result was amazing to say the least, especially when the company added a set of chromed

This flamed New Beetle matches Randy Zelany's other car, an original Beetle!

17 inch Alba multi-spoke alloy wheels. In a flash, McKennas turned a head-turner into a neck-twister!

The flame paint job theme has seemed to catch on across the country, with another owner of a black New Beetle having his car painted with orange flames, to match his 1961 Beetle. Have you got a white New Beetle? Well how about candy purple flames with anodised purple five-spoke alloy wheels? Too late, that has already been done! What about using the old Herbie theme on your white New Beetle, with a red and blue stripe right over the car and the famous number 53 on each door and across the bonnet? Too late, that's been done too! Brian Burrows, a VW event organiser, enthusiast and owner of a World Record holding drag racing Beetle, was the first to sneak a New Beetle out of Canada and into Britain. Having the first New Beetle in the country wasn't enough – he also wanted to be the first to race a New Beetle in competition. The car arrived in Britain on Wednesday 25th April. By Thursday, the car was being drilled to fit a fire extinguisher and battery cut-off switch. Then Brian had it sign-written and striped. Having planned the whole thing out way in advance, he had already secured S 53 as his racing number in the Street Class Championship of the British Volkswagen Drag Racing Club, so the Herbie number is official. The car was then driven to the Avon Park raceway where, on the Saturday morning, it became the first New Beetle in competition. The car covered the quarter mile in 18.37 seconds, which was nothing amazing. However, consider the owner's manual for a minute: 'During the first few operating hours, the engine's internal friction is higher than later when all the moving parts have been broken in. How well this break in process is done depends to a con-

siderable extent on the way the vehicle is driven during the first 600 miles. As a rule of thumb: Do not use full throttle. Do not drive faster than three quarters of top speed. Avoid high engine speeds.' Brian clearly followed these instructions to the letter...

Brian Burrows' Herbie was the first to be raced

The VW Adventure

Another New Beetle first was The VW Adventure, a journey which followed the famous Route 66 from California to New York. This was the brainchild of Blue Nelson, who, as mentioned earlier, went to the launches in L.A. and Vancouver. He got together with fellow vintage VW enthusiast Eric Meyer, owner of a shoe company called Simple, and the adventure began. The journey was covered by many local newspapers along the way, and updates were posted on a VW Adventure Web Site. Blue Nelson shipped the silver car – which has been a test bed for many prototype accessories – over to Britain in August 1998 for the second part of the VW Adventure. Blue now plans to drive the car around Europe, and hopefully the rest of the world.

By the summer of 1998, performance modifications started to appear on New Beetles at VW events across America. Companies such as Autobahn Designs, or ABD, brought out rear spoilers which mount below the rear window along with small additional spoilers to fit to each corner of the front bumper. ABD also looked at engine tweaks and enhancements. Instead of the standard air box, ABD offered a high-flow foam element-type filter. The smooth plastic engine cover with VW logo and 2.0 emblem was re-moulded by ABD in carbon fibre, which gave the stock engine a racy look. ADB also

Kristen Short from Las Vegas and her supercharged New Beetle

offer a range of higher lift camshafts and will continue to develop products for the New Beetle.

The most recent New Beetle products which have hit the market have include Wolf car covers, heat protective dash mats, 'bras' which fit either across the whole front of the car or just over the leading edge of the bonnet/hood, rear bumper spoilers, and front hoods with mean looking power bulges. It looks like the after-market options for the car will be huge business. It is predicted that VW itself will bring out some exciting accessories.

Of course, there is always VW's 1.8T-engined model, which VWOA have scheduled for launch at Detroit 1999. The 1.8 Litre twenty valve turbocharged unit is the same award-winning base engine used in the Audi A4, Passat and Golf 4. At 5,700rpm the engine produces 150bhp, adding 45bhp over the stock 2.0 Litre petrol engine, which produces 115bhp at 5,500rpm. The new engine will push the maximum top speed up to 126mph. Although at the time of writing the name has not been definitely settled, the 1.8T engined car may well end up being referred to as the New Beetle GTi.

Rumours of four wheel drive systems linked to either VR5 or VR6 engines have also been circulating. For some New Beetle owners waiting for performance models is not an option. This is where a company in Hermosa Beach, California, aptly named 'Dr. Boltz', comes into play. The company specialise in street and racing upgrades for VW, BMW and Porsche cars, but saw the market for New Beetle upgrades. Dr. Boltz started with the car it called Project Number 1, which was a turbocharged 2.0 Litre model producing 200bhp. The installation was designed to be a very neat fit, and as you can guess, it made the New Beetle perform very well indeed. The turbocharger 'kit' is now on the market and will cost around $2000 plus fitting charges. You can not simply add another 85bhp to your New Beetle without thinking about doing a little extra work to the suspension, though. A set of upgraded springs and anti-roll bars are recommended, along with a set of 17 or 18 inch wheels with wider tyres.

The next project car to come from Dr. Boltz was a VR6 powered New Beetle, and Bo Bertillson, a regular contributor to VolksWorld Magazine who is based in California, was one of the first to take a

Dr. Boltz' 'first' VR6-powered New Beetle – note the rear bumper extension

test ride in the car. Once fitted, the VR6 power plant looks although it was installed at the factory, it fits in so well. The engine has been 'chipped' and has high flow intake and exhaust systems, and is said to push up the power output from 178bhp to around 200bhp. Whilst this is around the same output as the Dr. Boltz turbo kit, there is one extremely significant improvement over the turbo – the VR6 has far more power in the lower rev range.

The price of a full Dr. Boltz VR6 conversion with full suspension, body styling and those lovely looking 17 inch Momo wheels is approximately $60,000. This price is of course 'turn key,' which means that includes the cost of the original car itself. Rumour has it that the Wolfsburg design team have obtained themselves a nice, white Dr. Boltz VR6 New Beetle for examination and testing. Whether or not this is fact or fiction, it would be nice to think that VW would release a New Beetle VR5 or 6. We all know how it works with VW now – all you have to do is make enough noise about something and convince enough people, and they'll do it...

Ross Palmer's team was the first to circuit-race a New Beetle

Kristen Short's highly modified New Beetle – 1 FAT BUG!

The New Beetle isn't only causing a stir when comes to modifications. It is also becoming a cult vehicle, and with the already-mentioned New Beetle Club picking up steam very quickly, an enthusiast following is assured. VW event organisers are already adding New Beetle classes for owners who wish to show their customised cars to other enthusiasts, and some of the results of the customisation process look absolutely stunning.

On the 12th February 1998 VW said, 'In terms of the number sold, compared with its predecessor, the New Beetle will never be more than a niche vehicle – but in a niche all of its own.' Despite this somewhat cautious, even pessimistic assessment, the future certainly looks bright for the most sensational new car in modern motoring history.

Vehicle Data

Concept 1

Vehicle Dimensions

Length 3824mm

Width 1636mm

Height 1500mm

Wheel base 2525mm

Weight 907kg

Track F&R 1488mm

Front Over Hang 664mm

Rear Over Hang 636mm

Front Ground Clearance 178mm

Rear Ground Clearance 241mm

Engine/Motor Specifications

TDI Version:

Design . . . . Direct-Injection Diesel Four Cylinder

Displacement 1900cc

Maximum Power 66kw

Maximum Torque 202Nm

Transmission . . . . 5-Speed Ecomatic

Maximum Speed 180Km/h

Fuel Consumption 5.1 L/100km

Acceleration . . . . 12.8 seconds 0-100 km/h

Electric version:

AC Induction

Maximum Power	37kW
Maximum Torque	130Nm
Transmission	2-Speed Automatic
Battery Type	Na/NiCl
Battery Weight	260kg
Stored Energy	22kWh
Rated Capacity	90Ah
Load Voltage	248Volts
Maximum Speed	125km/h
Urban Range	250km

Hybrid Version TDI-motor/Electric-motor:

Design	Direct Injection diesel three cylinder/ AC Induction
TDI Displacement	1400cc
Maximum Power	50kW
Maximum Torque	140Nm
Transmission	5-Speed Semi-Automatic
AC Induction Max Power	18kW
Battery Type	Ni/MeH
Battery Weight	180kg
Stored Energy	10kWh
Rated Capacity	55Ah
Off-Load Voltage	180Volts
Max Speed TDI	165km/h
Max Speed AC	105km/h

New Beetle

Body, Chassis and Suspension

Type	Unitised construction, bolt on fenders
Front Suspension	Independent McPherson struts, coil springs, telescopic shock absorbers, stabiliser bar
Rear Suspension	Independent torsion beam axle, coil springs, telescopic shock absorbers, stabiliser bar
Service Brakes	Power assisted, dual diagonal circuits, 280mm vented front discs and 239mm solid rear discs
Anti-Lock Braking	Optional, all four wheels
Parking Brake	Mechanical, effective on rear wheels
Wheels	6 1/2 J x 16, steel, with full covers, 5 bolts
Tires	205/55R 16H all season
Drag Coefficient	0.38

Dimensions

Wheel base, in	98.9
Track Front, in	59.6
Rear, in	58.7
Overall Length, in	161.1
Overall Width, in	67.9
Overall Height, in	59.5
Ground clearance, in	4.2

	5-Speed manual	4-Speed Automatic
Transmission	5-Speed manual	4-Speed Automatic
Curb Weight, lb	2712	2,778
Payload, lb	992	936

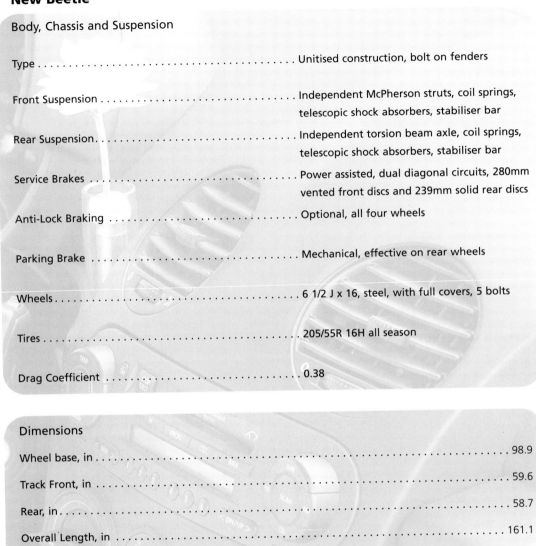

Fuel Consumption

Transmission	5-Speed manual		4-Speed Automatic	
Fuel	Gasoline	Diesel	Gasoline	Diesel
City, mpg *	23	41	22	34
Highway, mpg*	29	48	27	44

* May vary.

Engine

	Gasoline	Diesel
Type	2.0L, 4 Cyl, in-line	1.9L, 4-Cyl, in-line
Bore, in	3.25	3.13
Stroke, in	3.65	3.76
Displacement	1984cc	1896cc
Compression Ratio	10.0:1	19.5:1
Horsepower (SAE) @ rpm	115@5200	90@4000
Max. torque, lbs-ft @ rpm	122@2600	149@1900
Fuel Required	Regular Unleaded	Diesel

Engine Design

Arrangement	Front Mounted, Transverse
Cylinder Block	Cast Iron
Crank Shaft	Cast Iron, 5 main bearings
Cylinder Head	Aluminumalloy, cross flow
Valves train	Single overhead cam shaft, spur belt driven, 2valves per cylinder, maintenance free hydraulic lifters
Cooling	Water cooled, water pump, cross flow radiator, thermostatically controlled electric 2-speed radiator fan
Lubrication	Rotary gear pump, chain drive, oil cooler

Fuel/Air Supply. . . . . Sequential multi-port fuel injection (Motronic)

Emissions System . . . . OBD II, 3-way catalytcic converter with 2 oxygen sensors (upstream and downstream), enhanced evaporation system, Onboard Refuelling Vapour recovery (ORVR). TLEV (transitional low emissions vehicle) concept for California, Massachusetts and New York only

Transmission

5-Speed Manual	Gasoline	Diesel
1st	3.78:1	3.50:1
2nd	2.12:1	1.94:1
3rd	1.36:1	1.23:1
4th	1.03:1	0.84:1
5th	0.84:1	0.68:1
Reverse	3.60:1	3.60:1
Final Drive	4.24:1	3.89:1

4-Speed Automatic	Gasoline	Diesel
1st	2.74:1	2.71:1
2nd	1.55:1	1.44:1
3rd	1.00:1	1.44:1
4th	0.68:1	0.74:1
Reverse	2.11:1	2.88:1
Final Drive	4.88:1	3.63:1

Electrical System

Alternator, Volts/Amps. 14/90

Battery, Volts/Amps 12/60

Ignition . . . . Digital electronic, distributorless coil block,
with knock sensor

Firing Order 1-3-4-2

Capacities

Engine Oil (with Filter), qt 4.8

Fuel Tank, gal 14.5

Cooling System. qt 6.7

Steering

Type. . . . . Rack and Pinion, power assisted

Turns (lock to lock) 3.2

Turning Circle (curb to curb), ft. 32.8

Ratio 17.8:1

Interior

Seating Capacity . . . . Four

Head room front. . . . . 41.3 inches

Head room rear . . . . 34.6 inches

Shoulder Room . . . . 52.8 inches

Leg Room front . . . . 39.4 inches

Leg room rear. . . . . 33.0 inches

Exterior Features

Antenna	Roof mounted, amplified
Corrosion protection	26-step paint/corrosion process
Glass	Tinted
Horn	Dual tone horns
Lights, Front/Rear	Daytime running lights (DRL) upon start-up of vehicle headlights are engaged with reduced power, IP lighting, parking lights and taillights remain off. To engage all lights with full power the light switch must be turned to the 'on' position
	Halogen projector beam headlamps with clear polycarbonate lens
	Optional: Halogen projector lens front foglights
Mirrors	Body colour, power adjustable and heatable
Paint work	Solid or Metallic: Standard
Roof	Optional: Power glass sunroof, tilt and slide, tinted glass, with sunshade and power lock operated convenience closing feature
Alloy Wheels	Optional: 6 1/2 j x 16 inch alloy wheels, six spoke with VW logo hub cap and Anti theft wheel locks
Wipers/Washers	2 speed windshield wipers with variable intermittent wipe feature
	Optional: Heatable windshield washer nozzles (only in combination with heatable front seats)

Interior Comfort and Convenience Features

Air Conditioning . . . . CFC free with variable displacement A/C
compressor

Alarm/Anti Theft . . . . Anti theft alarm system for doors, hood,
trunk lid, radio and starter interrupt,
with warning LED in drivers' door top
sill and with activation 'beep'

Ashtray . . . . Dealer fitted option only

Assist handles . . . . Large assist handle in instrument panel
above glovebox, 2 rear assist straps on
'b' pillar

Clock . . . . Digital clock with blue display mounted
in central forward headliner

Cruise Control . . . . Optional: effective at speeds above 22mph

Defroster . . . . Electric heated rear window

Doors/Side panels . . . . Moulded door trim in leatherette with
upper sill moulding in exterior body

colour, black on vehicles with white exterior
Integrated arm rests in front door panels

Integrated arm rests in rear door/side panels

Floormats . . . . Front and rear carpet style, colour co-ordinated

Fuel filler . . . . Remote fuel filler release located on driver's
door inner, flap connected to fuel filler
neck to protect body

Instrument cluster . . . . Speedometer, tachometer, odometer, trip
odometer, fuel gauge, gear indicator (Automatic
transmission only), warning lights

Red illumination for controls (switches and
buttons), blue illumination for displays
(speedometer cluster and radio display)

headlights-on warning tone (upon opening of
driver's door when ignition key is removed)

Keys . . . . Valet Key

Lighting . . . . Combination interior and reading lamp located
in bottom sill of rear view mirror with time delay

Lighting continued	Glove box light
	luggage compartment light
Locks	Central power locking system (doors) with key operated closing feature for optional sunroof (if available), opening & closing feature for power windows (if so equipped) and selective unlocking at driver or passenger door
	Door mounted lock/unlock switches for central locking system
	Radio-frequency remote locking system with lock, unlock, trunk release and panic buttons on transmitter
Interior Mirrors	Driver and front passenger visor vanity mirror illuminated with cover
Power outlets	2 power outlets (SAE size) in centre console
Radio/Audio	AM/FM cassette stereo sound system with control capability for (optional) CD changer, theft-deterrent warning light and coding system. 6 speakers: 2 tweeters in 'A' pillar, 2 mid-woofers in front doors, 2 mid-woofers in rear quarter panel
	CD-changer preparation (cable from radio to luggage compartment)
Restraint System	Driver and front passenger airbag supplemental restraint system
	Front 3- point safety belts
	Height adjustment for front safety belts
	Rear outboard 3-point safety belts
	Emergency tensioning retractors for front safety belts
	Child seat tether anchorage system (rear seat)
	ALR, ELR (automatic locking retractor, emergency locking retractor) for front passenger and rear outboard safety belts, to secure child seat in place under normal driving conditions. Driver and front passenger side airbag supplemental restraint system
Seating, Front	Front seats, fully reclining, with height adjustment and 'ring style' headrests, easy entry system

integrated into front seat mechanism. Allows seat to move forward easily for access to rear seats

Optional: Heatable front seats (only with heated washer nozzles)

Seating, Rear . . . . One-piece folding rear seat

rear seat outboard ring style headrests

Steering wheel . . . . 3-spoke padded steering wheel

Optional: Leather wrapped steering wheel (only in combination with leather interior)

height adjustable and telescopic steering column

Steering wheel deformable upon impact

Collapsible steering column

Storage, interior . . . . Front door storage nets

Front passenger seatback magazine/storage pockets

Glovebox, lockable with interior shelf

Centre console with 3 front beverage holders and rear concealed beverage holder, colour co-ordinated

Trim (Details) . . . . Optional: Leather wrapped steering wheel

Optional: leather shift knob and boot (manual trans. only) and hand brake cover

Trunk/Cargo area . . . . Luggage compartment carpeting on floor, left and right side, rear of seat back

Upholstery . . . . 'Primus' velour seat fabric

Optional: Leatherette seat trim

Optional: Partial leather seat trim (seating surfaces)

Ventilation System . . . . Rear seat heat and A/c ducts, side window defoggers in IP Pollen/Odor filter for incoming air

Windows . . . . Manually operated windows

Optional: Electrically operated one-touch up or down (with pinch protection) and convenience close and open feature

Body Colours 1998

Solid	Metallic
White	Silver
Yellow	Green
Black	Bright Blue
Red	
Dark Blue	

Manufacturers Warranty

2 years/24,000 mile basic limited warranty

2 years/24,000 mile no charge scheduled maintenance

2 years unlimited mileage/distance 24 hour roadside assistance

10 years/100,000 mile Limited Power train Warranty

12 year unlimited mileage/ distance Corrosion Perforation warranty

VW Disclaimer: All equipment listed is subject to production related change or delayed availability.

What color do you dream in?

Drivers wanted. Ⓥ

Useful New Beetle Contacts

New Beetle Club
Randy Carlson
316 South Orange Avenue
Brea
California
92821

VolksWorld Magazine
Link House
Dingwall Avenue
Croydon
Surrey
CR9 2TA
England
http://www.linkhouse.co.uk
/volksworld

Dune Buggies and
Hot VWs Magazine
Wright Publishing Co., Inc.
PO Box 2260
Costa Mesa
CA 92626
U.S.A

Volkswagen Web Site:
http://www.vw.com

Volkswagen of America
information line:
1-800-444-8987.

Index